Single and Complete:
Alone and Content

Ndidi Ngwuluka

PLASELDI LIMITED

Nigeria

Single and Complete: Alone and Content

Copyright © 2015 by Ndidi Ngwuluka

Single and Complete: Alone and Content/Ndidi Ngwuluka

Plaseldi Limited
39 Yakubu Gowon Way,
Opp. Nitel, Jos, Plateau State,
Nigeria

Cover design by Wellington Kunaka
Book formatting and production by Dareprints
Editing by Jan Ackerson
Clipart by Presentermedia

Paperback ISBN 978-978-53766-0-9

eBook ISBN 978-978-53766-1-6

This is dedicated to all
women who have been
pressured against their will
and judgment

CONTENTS

FOREWORD

My early years of leading a church in Jos, Nigeria, brought me into contact with many young people between the ages of 19 and 35. Since those years, so much has changed in terms of narrative and belief system. This book is evidence of what has changed over the years, and I celebrate that success with so much excitement. I remember organizing and teaching marriage seminars, and the narrative was that God wants every young person to marry. In fact, getting married became synonymous with "settling down," another way of saying that "life has just really started." Those who were not married were considered not settled, or yet to start living. My associate and I had some fun with one of those many seminars, and called one of the sessions '*It is Better Not to Marry,*' a phrase taken from Jesus' disciples' response to His position on divorce. We discovered that most of our audience couldn't read between the lines, and attendance plummeted because this theme contradicts the narrative that marriage is a must, and it is God's will for all. I am delighted to see Ndidi writing about this, because she is highly qualified and I believe that she is paving the way for many others who have always wanted to do this but felt it would not be well-received. Moreover, there are married people who have written about singleness, but their audience has concluded that the writers can't understand because they don't know what unmarried people go through.

Ndidi's malleable heart has brought her to the point of allowing God to work on her. He has shown her that being unmarried is not a tragedy, as it is often perceived today.

This is the voice of one who can identify with the same feeling that many unmarried ladies go through. Nobody could better tell the story.

The fault that the Creator found with His creation when He said, "It is not good for man to be alone" was not limited to marriage. It has a wider application of humans' need for relationship and companionship with other humans

This book confirms my belief that whoever we were not created with, we can sure do without them.

I recommend it to all, both married and unmarried.

Dr. Oladotun Reju

Jos, Nigeria

Single and Complete:
Alone and Content

CHAPTER ONE

Introduction

I am single, but I am not cursed. I am single, but I am not sick. I am single, and it is okay.

I am single, and there is unrest around me precipitated by my singleness—unrest that insinuates that only marriage is the solution. Initially, when the pressure was high, the war raged within and without. I am single, and consciously or unconsciously, folks around me spent time and effort lecturing me about how abnormal singleness is. It used to be that the calmness within me slipped away as they lectured, but today, I smile and listen to them. Yes, I know better now. Sometimes with close friends, I choose to unsettle them by saying, "What if I'm called to be single? What if it's a gift?"

What is wrong with being single? Of all my friends, I'm the only one unmarried. It doesn't worry me, but it worries them. Some will never end our conversation without wanting to know "if something has happened." One of my friends always asks, "When are we coming for the wedding?" She gives me the impression that as long as I am not married, something is missing. I get the feeling she believes that as long as I am not married, I am not accomplished.

Why should marital status be used to define a woman? It is a foregone conclusion of those meeting me for the first time that I am a married woman, so I am addressed as Mrs. The pleasantries are: "How is your husband? How are the children?"

1

Then I have to correct them. Now don't get me wrong. I am not against marriage. It is indeed beautiful. Marriage is ordained by God, given for the purposes of companionship, sexual fulfillment, and procreation. I strongly believe that marriage should be held in high esteem. However, the emphasis in my society is not on marriage as an institution created by God, but on getting married as a requirement for attaining respect and recognition.

If a woman has not married for one reason or another, should she be made to feel miserable? Even when she is not worried, pressure is on her to worry. *It is not normal*, people say. What is abnormal about a woman choosing to be single? My society considers it abnormal. I am a Nigerian of the Ibo tribe. In Ibo land, most fathers who can afford it happily expect their daughters to obtain a university degree. After that first degree, marriage is expected. There are joys and celebrations when a daughter gets married. The daughter and her family unconsciously perceive this as an accomplishment. I have also interacted with some of the other tribes in Nigeria, and their ultimate desire for a daughter is also marriage.

I have spent time with friends in India, and it is also abnormal there for a young woman to be single. In fact, after interacting with some of them, I began to think the pressure to marry is stronger in India than in my country. Again I ask: what is wrong with a woman being single? In my culture, it is the man who seeks out a woman and proposes. It is not normal for a woman to propose, yet the pressure is more on the woman to marry. How sensible is that?

Adaeze completed her undergraduate program in chemical engineering. She had developed such a passion for chemical engineering that she thought it would be appropriate to proceed to obtain a postgraduate degree before seeking a job in the industry. After graduation, she took some time off to visit some friends and got back home two weeks later. As she walked into the sitting room, her father looked up from the newspaper he was reading. His face lit up when he saw her, and he said excitedly,

"Our chemical engineer!"

Adaeze is the first female chemical engineer in their clan.

"Your mother and I are proud of you. In fact, everyone in the clan who heard you had graduated with distinction is greatly pleased."

"Thank you, Dad. I'm happy, too. I enjoyed the program, and I am thinking of undertaking a master's program in chemical engineering."

Colour left her father's face, and the full smile was replaced with a frown.

Then he said, "Adaeze, you are a woman and the first daughter. The next thing you should be thinking about is marriage, not school."

Adaeze's heart tightened. Yes, she wanted to get married, but some years later. She hoped to get a postgraduate degree and to work for at least three years before getting married. Suddenly, her dream seemed on the verge of extinction. She could not go for the master's program without her father's support.

"But Daddy, the postgraduate program will offer me a better chance of getting a job." She tried to convince him.

Her father shook his head. "Hold on. Get married first. You can do that in your husband's house."

"But Daddy ..."

Her father's temper flared. "I am done training you. Go and get married!"

In fact, some fathers still have the perception that training a girl child is a waste of money, After all, she will get married, and the training will be of no benefit to her family. Is this true?

Training a girl child is not a waste of money. Some fathers I have interacted with allude to the fact that their daughters, though married, still provide for them. They are more likely to check in on their daughters than their sons. My sister is a college graduate, married, with a child, but she takes out time weekly to call our father. She was at the family home during the Christmas holidays, and she sends money to my father. Some daughters have built or refurbished their family homes, bought cars for their parents, and trained their siblings. Daughters, though married, remain attached to their families of origin and help out when and how they can. In Nigeria, we are oriented toward our extended families.

Most families with young girls groom them from childhood to eventually marry. If that does not happen, it becomes a major concern for the family and the young woman. Even the church does not help. A prayer of deliverance is organized, and demons are cast out. There are marriage seminars and conferences tagged, "It is my turn!" "God, I will not let you go!" "I must marry this year!" These activities by the church are mostly directed at women. Because of the intense pressure, women go to any length to get married, including getting pregnant, visiting a witch doctor or native doctor, or joining cults.

Women have been stereotyped, and they have accepted the stereotyping. Indeed, stereotyping may be less in some societies, but it is not completely gone anywhere. So women may continue to contend with this for a while. It is even worse when women themselves do same to their 'sisters'. So where do we start? With *us*. Let's talk to ourselves.

I am single, and I am fine with it. However, my singleness makes my friends uncomfortable. They are not contented with our conversations until the issue is brought up.

In December of last year, I decided to visit two old friends. Though we speak from time to time, we had not seen in a long time. I am about seven hours away from them by road

4

while they are one hour away from each other. I got to Ugomma's place, and then we drove to Stella's house together.

We went straight into her kitchen and helped ourselves to some rice and plantain. As we sat eating and listening to Stella tell us of the recent events in her place of work, Stella interrupted herself. Looking at me, she said, "You're looking fabulous! Who is the guy?"

I feigned ignorance. "What guy?" I asked.

"C'mon, for you to look this good, there has to be a guy in the picture! And don't tell me there isn't!" Stella had her eyes wide open and hands crisscrossed as she said that. Then she sat back, folded her eyes in a manner that implied, *I'm listening.*

Ugomma, who was initially digging into a chicken drumstick, dropped it on her plate, and as she licked her fingers, she looked at me, then at Stella. She chuckled. "There isn't a guy," she said.

Stella looked at me in disbelief. I thought, *Do we have to go down this road?*

"Look, Stella. I have a good job, and I am capable of taking care of myself!"

Stella rolled her eyes. "Ugomma and I also have good jobs as well. You need to settle down."

"But I am settled. I'm doing the things I love, and I'm happy! I have this Non-Governmental Organization where I'm working as a volunteer. Want to hear about it?" I responded, eager to change the topic.

Stella shook her head, "Poor girl. Anyway, I'm praying for you, and I know you'll meet someone someday."

Surely for a single woman, there should be more to her life. Singleness should not be merely endured, and it should not be viewed as a miserable and pitiable state. Singleness can be a gift or a calling, and should be respected. A single woman can be a marvel to her society as she makes a positive impact. Singlehood can be lived and enjoyed. Stay with me...

CHAPTER TWO
Singleness is a fun ride

I am single; I can walk, run, swim, fly, or do whatever I wish without feeling selfish.

"I'm happy being single!" said my new friend, Amita.

For the first time in my interaction with other women, I heard someone state that she was happy single. She gave this response after I had asked about her flatmate. Amita said her flatmate was never around on weekends; she was usually at her boyfriend's place. There were several long distance relationships amongst the women within our environment. I asked Amita if she was in a relationship. She said no, and then added that she was happy being single.

Although I had an inkling what she meant, considering that I am single, and I am maximizing every moment, I asked her why she was happy single. She said she liked the freedom it gave her. She was free to do whatever she wanted and to go wherever she wanted. This discussion was taking place on an outing that we had planned for days. Amita and Sara took me to explore Nariman Point, the 'Manhattan' of Mumbai.

Now on one of those days of planning, we single women invited another friend, Prisha, to come along.

"Prisha," I said, "Would you like to come to Nariman Point with us?"

7

Prisha looked uncomfortable. "I'd like to," she said, "but I have to ask my husband."

I knew that Prisha's husband was working many miles away, so I waited a bit. A few days later, I checked with Prisha again. "Can you come? What did your husband say?"

"I'm sorry, Ndidi," she replied. "I didn't get a chance to ask him. He's very busy. And I can't go without his permission."

Prisha had someone she was accountable to, someone she had to get permission from, even if a considerable distance separated them and there was no child to take care of. Consequently, without permission from husband, we left without her.

She was acting as a good wife should act, and that is certainly encouraged. However, this incident brings Amita's statement closer to home. I remember the day Amita was trying to pressure Prisha to join us. Prisha said that she was no longer free. She had someone over her and the other ladies did not.

Then Amita exclaimed, with her eyes wide open, "I have my father over me."

Now that got me thinking—do husbands have more control than fathers?

Let's ponder on this. I tell my father everything; he is aware of my plans and all my trips, even though I no longer live with him. I consult him on a lot of issues. So I understand Amita, who reminded Prisha she had someone over her— her father. However, though some of my plans are not approved by my father, I still go ahead, because I am convinced that my plans are good. If my father's objections made sense, I would comply.

Curious, I got a male perspective to this. My friend said he would not use the word 'control'. Men should not try to control their wives, as it would be counterproductive. He said the relationship between father and daughter is different from that of husband and wife. As a girl grows, the control of father over daughter wanes as she is deemed to be more and more responsible. A woman must be accountable to husband, but may choose not to be accountable to her father (as an adult and on her own).

I have been travelling a lot lately, and a friend, Clem, alluded to that. I got back from India and two days later I went to Clem's office, and we went for lunch. We placed our order, and as we waited, Clem asked, "So where is the next place you intend to visit?"

"Mauritius" I replied, feeling pleased with myself.

"Oh! So you actually have a place lined up!" he exclaimed with his eyes wide open.

"Yep."

Then he shook his head. "You are ever on the move."

I made a joking reply, "Let me do all the travels before someone says *sit down—you're not going anywhere,* and then I can console myself, knowing that I rocked my singlehood."

If you love travelling, why don't you do it now rather than sitting and feeling miserable? You don't need to whip up sentiments: "Oh I'm the only one left in my circle of friends to get married." "Oh, I'm approaching menopause." What a misery!

Although most societies say otherwise, getting married is not the main reason for the creation of women. In some areas, even if a woman has a dream, it is not encouraged. Some fathers do not bother about investing much in their daughters; after all, they will end up in their husbands' homes. So a woman is trained to believe if she hasn't

9

married, there must be something wrong with her. This prevents her from seeing the benefits of being single or the need to maximize the period of singleness.

I guess some women may be wondering what could be the benefits of being single in societies where single women do not receive respect, and families do not want any woman to be single. In fact, if you say you are celibate, some may say, "It is because no one has proposed to you that you have chosen celibacy." It is difficult for people to accept that a woman who is not a nun can choose to be single.

Single means having a singular focus.

A singular focus implies that one has an exceptional, remarkable or extraordinary attention to something. A singular focus is like an arrow that hits the bullseye; it is precise. Divided attention does not usually yield excellent results. Divided attention delays outputs and over time, interest is lost, and nothing gets accomplished. Projects are started but never finished. Once exciting and life-changing projects become abandoned along the way. When you are single, you can give extraordinary attention to a project. A singular focus will lead to sustainable success and a societal impact.

Men, including married men, succeed because of their focus. Most men believe that their job in the home is to bring in the money. To bring in the money, they focus on their business, and they usually succeed. Men have work engraved in their cells and tissues; a real man must work or have something to do, or he will be miserable.

Being single is an opportunity to have a pursuit without distractions. It provides the time, tenacity and precision to accomplish extraordinary things. How about spending your time and energy planning and executing projects, rather than wallowing in self-pity? I can assure you, it will be most rewarding.

Being single gives you an opportunity to pursue your dream vigorously.

I attended my college reunion and got chatting with some classmates. Apparently, Ida, Ijah, and Ojoma had kept in touch since we left college. Consequently, attention was on me as they wanted to know what I had been doing since graduation. Once I indicated I just completed a doctoral degree, the sentiments began:

"I would love to go for my Ph.D., but my children are tender and need my attention," said Ojoma.

"Just my thoughts," Ijah added. "If I travel out of the country for a Ph.D., who will take care of my children?"

"I love traveling and writing about my travels, but now I'm married. It's no longer possible to travel often," Ida interjected.

"I love research, but I cannot spend long hours in the laboratory. I used to imagine myself as an inventor, but now I have many demands on my time, and I've shelved my desires." Ojoma looked as if she was imagining it as she spoke.

"Lucky you, Ndidi. Now that we are married, we can't afford to be selfish. We have to think of the good of the family," Ida moaned.

"Yes," Ojoma and Ijah agreed obviously with mixed feelings.

Rightly said! Some of them get to the point of desperation and depression—feeling like nobodies—and they begin to blame their families. Some of my friends jumped right into marriage after school, not having a full grasp of what marriage is all about, only to realize that the music is not so easy to dance to. However, there are some who handle their situations maturely. They sacrifice some years for their

children, and once the children are grown, they pick up their dreams and run with them. Unfortunately, others get intimidated, allowing age to defeat them and burying their dreams forever.

As a single person, you can pursue your dreams without tapering them to suit another person's plans or expectations.

So, single lady, instead of spending all your time and energy worrying and bemoaning your state of being single, use the moment and accomplish some desires. Ask yourself, *what have I always dreamed of as a child?* Then run with it. Marriage can happen along the way.

Being single gives you time to discover and know yourself.

While we are under our parents' care, we are on automatic pilot. We wake up in the morning, do house chores, go to school, come back, do school homework, do more chores, and watch TV. Our parents supply most of our needs, and there is little we understand about life and ourselves. However, when we move away from our parents and begin to live on our own, our parents finally begin to make sense, and we begin to see ourselves in a different light. We start to understand and to value the disciplines they gave us. We begin to understand our parents' frugality and managerial skills.

A friend, Nina, once told me about her friend, Judy. A few weeks after Judy got a job and moved out of her parents' home, she exclaimed to Nina, "Tissue paper is expensive!"

The challenges of life reveal ourselves more and more to us. Being single and away from home for a while helps us to come to terms with several things. We begin to understand the difference between want and need, which then helps us in the choice of a life partner. Many women have married the wrong man for one reason—they had not yet discovered who they are. Who you are ought to influence who you want to live with for the rest of your life.

So take the time of being single to understand who you are. What are your likes and dislikes? What are your aspirations and dreams? These will help you to make the right choice. Then you can look beyond outward appearances and begin to seek the beauty inside.

You have time to commit to a societal cause.

Our society needs people of influence, movers and shakers and revolutionists. These are not the exclusive rights of men. Men and women can complement each other in effecting changes in our world. Men come with their perspectives, and women come with their perspectives, creating a holistic approach to solving a problem. So why whine and complain to all who have ears about how time is racing past you—how all your friends have left you in the dust—when you can devote yourself to a cause? You can spend your time and energy carving your name on hearts by taking up a societal problem and proffering a solution.

I am a volunteer with a Non-Government Organization whose thematic areas are democracy and governance, public health, environmental practices, economic empowerment, educational development and community development. However, our strongest areas are the provision of medical services in rural areas, and educational and economic empowerment of vulnerable groups. I feel blessed and privileged to be part of such a community service.

You have time to learn new skills.

What skills do you want to acquire? Now is the time! You will have enough challenges and things to do when you get married, so do what you have to do now. How about improving your communication skills? You will need to do so if you end up getting married. One of the major reasons for failure in marriage is a lack of communication skills. Communication will also help you at your place of work.

How about taking an online course, running a blog, or equipping yourself with skills that can help you work from home, should you become a stay-at-home mum? Make a note of skills you would like to acquire and begin the process of acquiring them.

I am making quite some progress in my career. Recently, I spoke to myself. *Look, you don't have to wait until you are called upon to head a team or department before you acquire leadership skills. If you acquire the skills now, you make fewer mistakes when you lead.* So I registered for an online course on leadership.

It gives room for creativity.

Solitary does have its advantages. You can focus on finding artistic expression. Some writers confess that they write best when they are alone, with few distractions. Hence, most of them prefer the early hours of the morning for writing. Painters, architects, and sculptors, I presume, feel the same way. Of course, I am also aware that some may prefer people-watching in the park. However, even in that park, some still don't want to be interrupted or engaged in a conversation. Being alone may shut down noises and allow ideas to exude from within. Our imaginations can run wild, and we can harness our creativity.

You are more effective at work.

Now is the time to take your career to its zenith. When you marry, your family will have to come first and career second. Society may advise you to slow down, so you do not ward off men by your successes. I have not taken that advice.

As a single, when you make any career decision, it will affect only you. I remember when I was in a relationship, and I was talking about going for a postgraduate program. The man was not supportive; he wanted me to have children first. I tried to explain to him that post-graduate work would be more challenging if I had children. Also, I was going to stall in my career because there would be no promotion without the postgraduate program. He refused to understand how frustrating it would be to remain at one level for years. I even pleaded that I was ready to try both—the postgraduate program and having babies. He still refused. That would have been a trying marriage because my personal and career development was of no importance to him.

So push your career as far as you can while you are single.

The challenges make a better YOU.

Because you are alone, you are compelled to get a lot of chores done. The more you do, the better you are at it. Single women may end up learning how to take care of their cars, with no husband to do it.

I take my car to the mechanic, and I have learnt some parts of the vehicle: shafts, shocks, brake pads, master cylinder. I now know that tires have expiry dates. Before, I used to think tires could be used until they were worn. Now I know I have to check for expiry dates before I buy tires, and I can change the tires, too. I know how to change the fuse of a stabilizer. I wash and polish my car myself; even my mechanic is impressed.

I can go on and on about the things I have learnt to do simply by being single and living in a house of my own. Knowing how to do things—as tiring as they may be—builds confidence and independence.

A time to give attention to yourself

You can attend to *you*. It is an unwritten law that women are to be self-sacrificing. Self-sacrifice is a virtue, but most women sacrifice at the expense of their health. Hence, they can die or become prematurely disabled because they are busy taking care of everyone else in the family but

15

themselves.

If you are in a relationship, you will have to take out time for that relationship. Between your demanding job and your partner and children, there is little time left for you to attend to yourself. Sustaining a healthy relationship requires time and effort, mentally, emotionally, financially, and psychologically. You need to study behavior to help you communicate and relate better. That requires time. However, being single affords you the opportunity and time to learn to take care of yourself. You are free to visit the spa, buy yourself good clothes, and spend money on personal development.

Singleness adds flexibility to your schedule.

You can do spontaneous things like wake up one morning and decide to drop off your resignation letter, which would have been hard to do if you had to tend to your family. You can leave from work to the airport on a Friday, and you don't have to get an approval or go home to get some things sorted out so your family can manage in your absence. You can just be spontaneous, without having to plan or consider the implications on those who depend on you.

Your money at your discretion

When you have a family or even just a husband, what to do with your money is planned with others in mind. However, as a single, you can do whatever you want with it. It can go for career development, which may not be possible if a family is involved. When I went for my program, I would save my salary through the year so as to pay the next year's school fees. I doubt if that would have been possible if I had a family. Not having a family afforded me time to focus on study, rather than struggling to make ends meet as well.

Have time to enjoy your family of origin.

As a child, you probably fought with your siblings, and you may have felt that your parents did not love you because they disciplined you. As an adult, you now understand whatever they did was out of love. You can use this time of singleness to get to know them, and to enjoy their company.

It is such fun when my siblings and I gather back at the family house. We banter into the early hours of the morning. Each time, I feel, "Oh, how I miss these guys!" When you marry, you will be too busy with your new family. Enjoy your family of origin now.

And socialize...

Family ties and other commitments that come with marriage leave little room for socializing. Now is the opportunity to have fun relating with as many people as possible. Engage in the social networking that may help advance your career now. It's healthy for you; you will be saner, less lonely, and you will live longer.

And disadvantages...

There are times when I come home tired and burdened, wishing I could talk to someone. If that happens to you, you can get a flatmate, or make calls, or visit friends.

If you are sick or old, you may be worried that there is no one to do the basic necessary chores for you, but friends will come around to help out. Besides, who says your family will really be available to help?

Nella is in her sixties and leaving alone. Her son is in another city. I went to spend some days with her, and as we sat watching the television, I asked, "How is James?"

She sighed and did not respond initially. She fixed her eyes on the television screen. I was certain she heard me. So I decided to give her time, wondering what could be wrong.

She sighed again and replied, "James must be fine. He hardly calls and when I call it goes into voicemail. I have not heard from him in months."

Single women are not respected, you may say. However, I am glad this mentality is changing in some quarters. Besides, you can earn respect by your influence and by being extraordinary

Seriously, for every disadvantage, there is a way round it.

CHAPTER THREE
Marital status does not define you.

I am first an individual who prefers to be known for who I am and not for any condition.

As the pressure to get married accelerated beyond my capacity to withstand it, I began to consider settling for less. What do I mean? I was dating someone, and I didn't particularly like him, but I went ahead because the heat was on. I got to a point where I began to think that people around me were more interested in me being 'Mrs.' than in my happiness. No one was thinking of the possibility of marriage snuffing the life out of me. Previously, I could apply the brakes to the accelerated pressure, and I would have some peace for some time. I think some years later, my 'uncoupled' phase was freaking out people around me more than it was 'chilling' me. At that stage, the hydraulic fluid must have leaked out, because all efforts on the brakes proved abortive. I began to give in to the pressure to marry.

I felt resigned. *I will marry this guy*, I thought, despite the incompatibilities staring at me. His verbal and emotional abuses were raining on me daily, yet I was tagging along. Over time, I'd lost the strength to resist the pressure to marry, and I was tired. I decided, *Okay, all people want is for me just to get married. Fine! I'll marry him, and two months later, I'll walk away. At least the story will change from "she has refused to get married" to "she was married."* But something stopped me in my tracks. I heard in my spirit, *Will God applaud that?* Getting married just to get people off my back is an insult to the institution of marriage.

Besides, my people would not be affected in any way by such an act. I would be bearing the brunt of it all—the dents, the emotional stress, the estrangement.

Then I read this:

And don't be wishing you were someplace else or with someone else. Where you are right now is God's place for you. Live and obey and love and believe right there. God, not your marital status, defines your life (1 Corinthians 7:17).

Where I am right now is God's place for me. Where you are NOW is God's place for you. That may or may not change. If it changes and you become coupled, great! At least you will be happy that you did not waste the single period.

Yes, I am single, but instead of being miserable and desperate, and instead of succumbing to detrimental pressures, I shall live, obey, love, believe and hope. Above all, although society will want to define me by marital status, I don't have to accept that. It is my maker who defines me, and he loves me even as a single woman.

When I had this understanding, I was liberated for life! Seriously, all the pressures rushed out of me. I felt them leave like a goat scrambling out of the road at the toot of a horn.

Defining people by their marital status is an abnormality that people accept as normal. However, that does not make it normal. Refuse to be defined by your marital status.

How can I be effectively described by marital status? Such definition misses my specific nature and qualities; nevertheless, it happens. How can a person be effectively described by her relationships? If she is not in a 'relationship', then something is odd about her. However, before a woman gets into a relationship or marries, she is first an individual, a personality. Does it mean a personality can only be defined if and when she is married? Yes, that is the marital status the society, in general, embraces.

Interestingly, woman have been sold this myth for many years. A girl child is born, she grows up, and her final destination is marriage. All her life, she is groomed for marriage. This affects some girls; they are dreamless, with no aspirations. "Why bother? After all, I am born for someone else!"

Even when they dare to dream, they are shut up. You hear such words as "Which man will permit that? Forget it!" Girls grow up, and all they aspire to accomplish is marriage.

I remember the joke while we were growing up. With the tradition of bride price, friends would crack jokes about being sold or being up for sale or being on the shelf. And when it seems that marriage has been delayed for a particular person, you hear such things as "Be careful, so you are not forgotten on the shelf" or "You will soon expire." According to society, this is all women are good for: to be handed over to men. If that does not happen, the family is worried and friends are on the edge, working hard to change the woman's status. If you are clocking forty or upwards and you have not heard 'just get married', then you are in a good place.

If you are single, inevitably the matchmaking and the pairing starts. Your fashion statement has to change. If you are conservative in your dress, throw that to the bin and dress sexy. You have to flaunt it to attract him. Let's not forget the quest to change your personality as well—the 'training' to hide the real you so you can find 'Mr. Right', who would be threatened by the real you.

Imagine that you are one of those strong-willed women who refuses to fold her hands and wait for Mr. Right. You have had many professional and personal developments, but you are advised not to tell men about your accomplishments and your aspirations. Ambitious women are told not to intimidate men and scare them away, so play small and get married.

My question is, what happens when you marry and reveal the real you? Would a man be intimidated? Wouldn't there be friction in the home? Wouldn't he feel betrayed? The bottom line is, *be hypocritical and get the guy*. Otherwise, you will be incomplete. It doesn't matter what you have accomplished, or the impact you have made in society—as long as you are not married, there is a 'but' in your life. In some societies, the 'but' is so amplified that if a woman is not strong, she will also believe the 'but'. She begins to do all sorts of things to change the 'but'. She is desperate and ready to settle for less.

When a woman is desperate, she is no longer thinking straight. Even when the signs are present that a relationship would not work, she chooses to ignore them. Some women are so desperate that they foot the wedding bills 100%, including buying the suit for the groom. I wonder what makes these women think that when they marry, the problem will end. It will not—but she has opened a whole new drum of challenges. Then she may begin to realize that the title 'Mrs.' was obtained at a cut-throat price. She would have been better single.

Some wives are abused, but because 'Mrs.' is better than life, they stay in an abusive marriage—and they die in it. Yes, I agree that some stay because of the children. But in some cases, even the children are abused. Are you sure you are really staying because of the children, or are you afraid of what society would say if you walked out?

Some people don't think a single woman can have a healthy relationship with a married man. Once you are talking with a married man and people notice that you are at ease, attention is on you. In fact, some people will be bold enough to tell you to back off, or they'll take it upon themselves to advise you to stay away from this married man. Such a friendship may affect the chances of single men considering you. But what if the man is a colleague at work and you are teammates who have to work together every day?

I wish society would understand that God gives the gift of single life to some and the gift of marriage to others. If you find someone to marry you, be happy. If you don't get married, be happy, too. Marriage is just a section of your whole life. Why frustrate the other sections simply because you may not have fulfilled one section? The truth is, **we need to understand that neither marriage nor singleness is inferior to the other**.

Who defines you?

God defines you! God's definition of me may seem far-fetched, but God does not lie. He knows that it is possible for me to be who he says I am. I may seem all muddled up, but he loves me all the same and will nurture and nudge me to be who he says I am.

A while ago, I wrote an article called, *The Woman! Who Defines Her?* I'd like to append that here.

The Woman! Who defines her?

She is a housekeeper who must maintain the smooth running of a home—hers or otherwise.

She is a sex object, available for the man, whether she likes it or not, whenever he wants sex.

She is a weakling, and she should be treated as such.

She is only somebody respectable when she marries.

She should be seen but not heard, and must submit at all times, even if the situation is dead wrong.

She is Figure 8, with right and proportionate curves in the right places. Otherwise, she has to check in for re-shaping.

These are a few definitions that society has given women when they have not accurately defined themselves. When the pressure gets too much, some women make drastic decisions that have unpalatable consequences. They resign to society's definitions of womanhood and pressure fellow women to do so as well.

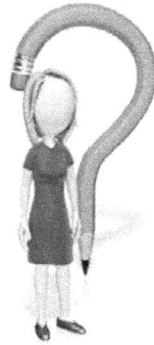

Woman! Who are you?

Who can rightly define a woman? Who knows her well enough to define her? The woman does not know herself well enough. If she did, she would not submit herself to inaccurate definitions.

Surely, there is one who has an accurate definition of the woman—her creator. The one who formed her is the only one who can accurately define her. Only from him should the woman accept her definition.

Due to societal and peer pressures, women try to be who they are not. She wishes she is where she should not be, without understanding that she is where her creator wants her to be at that moment. She ought to be content and to be happy where she is. She should delight in who she is, but how can she delight in who she is if she does not know who she is?

Society defines women by their marital status. She accepts this definition and goes into panic mode when she is not married. In panic mode, she makes wrong choices and consoles herself that at least she is married. But her creator says, "Your marital status does not define you. I define you!"

The world views her as a sex object and entices her with money in exchange for sex or "love". So she gives away her body carelessly. Of course, in some cases she is violated against her will, but her creator says, "Her body is the temple I dwell in. I bought it with a price, and it should not be vandalized."

She is not to be heard, but her creator says, "My daughters shall prophesy" (Joel 2: 28 KJV).

She is adorned in tenderness and peace, she is trusted, and she has a quiet and gentle spirit, living in fear of her creator only.

When she can't take the pressure anymore, she rebels. "Enough of these pressures! It is time that I run my own life. It is time I prove to the opposite sex that I am strong; I am your equal; I can be independent of you, and I can be in control!"

But her creator says, "Let me be in the driver's seat. Relinquish control to me; yield your lifestyle to me and let me be in charge of you. Let me be your Lord, manager, protector, friend and soulmate." Her creator says, "Drop all definitions given by those who do not know you. Drop all definitions given by those who were not there when I formed you. My princess, let me define you!"

But how does the woman obtain her definition from her creator?

Jesus asked his disciples, "Who do people say I am?" They reeled off names they'd heard from other people, names such as John the Baptist, Elijah, Jeremiah. But Jesus wanted to find out who the disciples thought he was. Peter spoke up and gave an accurate definition—the Christ, the Messiah, the Son of the Living God. When Peter gave Jesus his accurate definition, Jesus was very impressed. He said, "Now I will tell you who you are!" You are Peter, a rock" (Matthew 16:16-18).

Woman, your definition is in knowing God for yourself. You don't relate to him based on who people say He is. You relate to him based on who you have discovered he is. In discovering God for yourself, you discover you. You obtain your definition.

Society will define you inaccurately, but God will give you a perfect definition that exactly describes who you are.

Walk away from society's definitions; walk to and with God; then you shall know who you are. Make knowing God your singular pursuit, and watch him tell you who you are. In your walk with God, ask him, "Who am I?" When you know who you are—be who you are.

Who am I?

I am African royalty with a cultural influence.

I am a star recharged by God's presence, shining on paths for people to follow.

These are some of God's definitions of me.

So you—woman reading this—who does God say you are?

I am the creature who delights her creator.

When we know who we are, we will no longer allow society to dictate inaccurately how we should live or who we should be. Then we are free to enjoy and to maximize the period of singlehood as God has permitted. We are free to be single if we choose to be. We are free to be who God says we are. Where I am right now (being single) is God's place for me.

26

CHAPTER FOUR

Happiness is rooted in you

As a child, I was happy despite my challenges; surely as an adult, I can also be happy despite my challenges

Have you ever felt bored and decided to call up a few friends, only to learn that they had other plans? You feel so alone, and all sorts of negative thoughts begin to flood your mind; you begin to pity yourself, and you may even start weeping. You feel left out and forgotten. You compare yourself with others, feeling they are better off.

Then you think that maybe marriage would make you happy. Your husband would fulfill all your fantasies about coupling and attend to all your needs. Well, here is the news—you will also be doing that for him. Marriage is not a destination where there is a person who is at your beck and call. In that ideal scenario, as soon as you arrive home, he gives you a glass of water, then he guides you to the bathroom so you can freshen up. He serves you the meal he has cooked. Once you are done, he gives you a soothing massage and then puts you nicely to bed. Unfortunately, there is no way that will happen because both of you got there at the same time—and you are to serve each other.

Marriage is a journey of knowing, understanding, serving and making sacrifices that will produce a tried, tested and refined couple enjoying their lives amidst the challenges. It is an institution that requires people to be selfless. When you are focused on someone else making you happy, you tilt the pendulum of marriage, and it becomes imbalanced. When you are planning to depend on someone for your happiness, you add pressure on your partner, which further ensures that happiness will elude you.

Learn to delight in yourself and enjoy your own company. When you don't like yourself, you find yourself always wanting to run away from you, which means you will always want to be in someone else's company, or burying yourself in work.

Happiness comes from within. Better still, choose a higher disposition—joy. Some people debate the difference between happiness and joy. I perceive happiness as conditional while joy is unconditional. When the going is good, I am happy. When the going spins out of control, and there are obstacles to surmount, I am unhappy. However, as I mature, I am beginning to sense a calm disposition—joy— even when things spin out of control.

I am learning to be carefree in my creator's careful hands. I am not there 100%, but I am getting there. I am certain of these things: God loves me and will not withhold anything good from me, and he is interested even in the tiniest details of my life. He does not take his eyes off me. When unpalatable things happen, I look to him because I know they did not escape him. From interactions with him, I am accepting that all things—good, bad and ugly—work together for my good. Sometimes when unpleasant things happen, I realize that I am calm. Yes, I wish it was a smooth sail, and of course, there is a feeling of displeasure, but at the same time, I can give thanks to God. Only eternal joy, a gift from our Maker, can produce such a disposition. I don't deny the unpleasant situation, but I am not overwhelmed by it.

Recently, I was faced with a situation that cost me money, time, and effort, and yet it was not successful. I had been invited to an important event: a L'Oreal/UNESCO regional fellowship for women in science in Sub-Saharan Africa, all expenses paid. I was in India, and the event was in South Africa, and I needed a visa. I attempted to apply from India;

however, the required documents specified that I must have been in India for six months to obtain the visa. When it became obvious that I could not apply from India, I rescheduled my trip so as to get back to Nigeria and apply before the date of the event. On the day of departure, the Ethiopian airline was delayed in Mumbai, and I missed the connecting flight from Ethiopia to Nigeria. The next flight was two days later, so I spent two days in Addis Ababa. Then there was the weekend, and the event drew near. I was able to apply for the visa, but I still did not receive the passport until after the event. The event was the entire reason I had left India earlier than planned, but I still did not make it.

As I thought about it, I said to myself, "Life is an adventure; embrace it." I did try to look at the good side of it. While in Ethiopia, I did not stay in the hotel, sulking. The first day, we took a drive, and I saw a bit of Addis Ababa. Then a friend arranged for someone to take me out the next day to watch cultural dances in a traditional setting. I loved it, and I almost forgot I was stranded in Addis Ababa. It was not what I bargained for, but I made the most of it with the help of friends.

We make a move, we take a plunge, and sometimes we are even faced with an unexpected outcome. What do we do? Sulk? Be miserable? Or accept that life is an adventure and take it all in stride?

Some women are waiting for marriage before they can have fun and live their lives to the fullest. Things do not always turn out the way we expect. Marriage may present an uncertain, unexpected outcome. Remember, marriage has inherent challenges that ought to be handled maturely for sustainability. Desperate women who wait in earnest to get

29

married plunge into depression as they find themselves aging without a husband. This should not be so. Being single is not a curse, and single women should not be viewed as afflicted. We can be single and happy. We can be alone and joyful.

Being alone does not have to translate to being lonely. Being alone simply means going solo without companionship.

Joy is God's gift. As we delight in him, his joy radiates in and through us. To cultivate being joyful as a single person, interact consistently with your maker, and be busy in your passions. Be content in whatever phase or situation you find yourself. Be thankful, be optimistic, be meditative, and be outgoing.

Our earthly predisposition is to see the things that are not working. In such situations, we tend to forget those that have worked out perfectly without us lifting a muscle or without many obstacles. We need always to be thankful and to count our blessings. As we do that, we become hopeful that the hopeless situation may turn around. Even if the situation remains hopeless, look carefully, and you will see reasons to thank God.

After two futile attempts at trying to get a student visa to study in the UK, I decided to go to South Africa. As I began to process that change of plans, God's intervention began to unfold. When I got to South Africa, I realized that God was trying to save me some financial headaches (as an international student, studying in the UK is more expensive). I also found out my supervisor's laboratory in South Africa was comparable to any standard laboratory in the UK. In fact, my discussion with some who had studied in the UK made me realize I would be exposed to more skills in South Africa. I think I came out of South Africa better than I would have come out of the UK. Meanwhile, I felt miserable when I did not get the UK visa.

What I don't have now, I don't need. When I need it, God

will provide. If I am single, I ought to be content and thankful to God, who sees into the future and orchestrates my life. I shall be happy in my present phase. Should it become a permanent phase, I shall still be thankful and invest in lives around me, making an indelible impact.

Making friends and sustaining relationships goes a long way in keeping us on the road of joy and happiness. We need friends to encourage us, comfort us, and pull us out of depression, as well as to boost our self-esteem. Making and sustaining good and productive friendships is worth the time and effort. Friends can motivate you to learn new skills and keep you busy. They can help get your mind off the pressure of *I am getting old...I need to get married... when will I get married...I am the only one left.*

If you are eager to get married and it is not happening, you need to seek out friends to help you live a fruitful life as you seek to marry. A strong support from friends helps us to cope with the stress placed upon us by ourselves or by society. They will also prevent you from making wrong decisions regarding a life partner. Of course, you have to choose your friends wisely because some friends can be sources of stress.

So don't lock up yourself, thinking it is only when you get married that you will be happy. Choose to be happy. Yes, happiness is a choice; it should not be tied to certain happenings or accomplishments. Alter your attitude towards your single life and choose to be happy. Be appreciative of the opportunities being single has offered you. Be filled with joy!

CHAPTER FIVE

Stop feeding the life suckers

Life suckers are products of our reactions to events in our lives.

What if you are destined to be single? Seriously, marriage is not for everyone, just as being alone is not for everyone. If you desire marriage but for one reason or the other there has been a delay in that coming to fruition, you may need to be careful and stable. Otherwise, you may find yourself out of control and driving down unwanted roads. Single life should not be a life of misery. It should not be a life-sucking period. Make the most of it, so that when you finally meet the right guy, you will not regret your single life. If you don't manage your single period effectively, you may make the wrong choice and find marriage more miserable.

The single life becomes easier and more productive when you get rid of some life suckers, most of which come from self-preoccupation. Granted, your background may have precipitated self-preoccupation, but you can choose to re-invent yourself. When you daydream about yourself, what do you see? Most of us see an exemplary personality—a person of positive influence—but we make no deliberate effort to bring that to fruition. I am a firm believer that *if I can dream of it, then it is possible.* It is possible to walk away from all that seems not right about your past and walk into a future of possibilities and become that person you dream to be. People have done it; so can you. Just get rid of the life suckers.

Compulsive preoccupation with self is a dead end. Why do that to yourself? Focus on self can swing two ways. In one extreme, you are full of yourself and have a disregard for others, feeling as if all good things should come your way. When something good happens to someone else and not to you, you plunge into the road of negativity and hostility at a fast speed. You begin to voice your thoughts with hostility, making others want to keep their distance. Your baggage increases. You had a superiority complex—which actually comes from insecurity. Then as you continue in this direction, you swing into an inferiority complex.

You withdraw into your shell. You get to an intersection and refuse to move. You are filled with uncertainties. You are afraid to take any risk. You become very cautious, paralyzed by what people will say about you or your actions. You choose to remain at the intersection, forgetting that there are people behind you waiting to go through. Perhaps while you were growing up, you were so put down that you believed it. Even when fresh air with a hint of lavender comes your way, you are not conscious of it. All you can perceive is the stench.

At this stage, your behavior has become more confusing, further keeping people away from you. Superiority and inferiority complexes are life suckers.

Low self-esteem propels one into inactivity. You imagine all the good things you can have and all you can accomplish. In your daydream world, they all come together. But of course, there is no courage and belief to translate those dreams into reality. You spend your time in the dream, rather than working towards its fulfillment.

No need pointing fingers at anyone. Your worst enemy to your progress is *you*. You may be saying that is not true—you were not responsible for the emotional, mental, physical, psychological and social abuses that have left an indelible impact on you. On the contrary, it may take time, but with determination and perseverance, a transformation can take place. You can change. There is no such thing as "that is the way I am" or "this is how I have been made to be". The biggest room ever is that of change. As the saying goes, change is the only constant. You can make a transforming change that will dazzle within and without, propelling you into a fruitful existence. However, you cannot do it on your own. God can! You become your worst enemy when you do not yield to him to heal and transform you.

Self-preoccupation and other life suckers can imprison you. However, focus on your creator, and God frees you to possess a limitless life. It brings you into a creative space where all things become possible.

I have had some negative things spoken into my life, but I have risen above them to the admiration of those who spoke those things. My confidence grew in the one who called me "My daughter, the apple of my eye and the chosen one" even when I did not deserve those names. I stepped away from those words, certainly not ignorant of my shortcomings, but trusting the one who has called me to be. Everything I am today and all I have accomplished came from him. If he can do it for me, he can do it for you.

How do you stop feeding the life suckers?

It is just simply three words: *Change your mindset.* Feelings and actions do not just happen; they emanate from our thoughts. The shackles and chains that are incapacitating you will break off when there is a switch in your thought pattern. So when you renew your mind, you starve the life suckers; they dry and fall off. Life suckers feed on negativism. As your mind is renewed, you shift away from negativism.

Now how does your mind get renewed? You cannot achieve this on your own. You need a higher power, for it is an easy tendency to conform to the cultures around you. There is also the tendency to succumb to the unhealthy and life-damaging demands placed on us. Here's the answer:

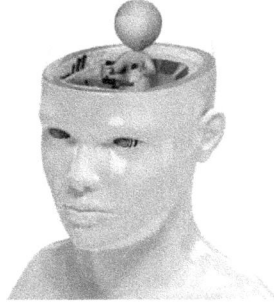

"Don't become so well-adjusted to your culture that you fit into it without even thinking. Instead, fix your attention on God. You'll be changed from the inside out. Readily recognize what he wants from you, and quickly respond to it. Unlike the culture around you, always dragging you down to its level of immaturity, God brings the best out of you, develops well-formed maturity in you" (Romans 12:2 - MSG).

I read this again recently, and it opened up even more to me. Sometimes the word of God means more when you are in a situation where it applies perfectly. My first inclination, when I am wronged, is to think of retaliating. A friend hurts me, and the first thought is to hurt back so that she will not do it again. Sometimes I deceive myself by saying, *I'm only retaliating so she will not do it to someone else.*

I have a friend who makes promises and does not keep them. I keep pointing this out to him. Now and then I find myself tempted to do same to him. *Let me pay him back in his own coin, so he knows how it feels.* However, as I spend time with the word of God and meditate on it, it encourages me to do the right thing. We are to love and forgive!

A few months ago, I got back to my neighborhood, having been away for a while. I was displeased to observe that some people have been irresponsible. The driveway gate needed repairs. I was made to understand it had been in such a state for a while. Was the problem waiting for me to solve it because I had solved it before? In fact, I would not have minded if someone had fixed the gate in my absence and asked to be paid for it. Then I began to think, *I should ignore the problem, just like the others.* The culture around me is selfish and individualistic. If I choose to ignore the damage, will I not be allowing the culture around me to drag me down to its level of immaturity? Jesus never shied away from responsibilities, nor did he allow the Pharisees to drag him down to their level of whitewashed religion. So as these thoughts re-echoed in me, I decided to have the repairs done.

To renew my mind, I fix my attention on God, refusing to fit mindlessly into the culture around me. As I focus on God, he changes me from the inside out. The change is sped up by me eagerly perceiving what he wants from me, and promptly conforming to it. I have my weak areas and sins I struggle with, and I get upset with myself for repeating those sins over.

I cried out to God because of my weaknesses, but one day, I sensed him saying, "Keep your gaze on me. Someday you will look back and see that those sins are no more." Now I understand that it may take a while for some sins to be no more. God is interested in the process of perfecting us. He is interested in us never giving up; we ought to keep rising each time we fall. We come to the realization that we have to be totally dependent on him for the transformation. So we have to gaze consistently on him and in the end we fully become who we behold—Christ.

We need to let Christ work in us, to reprogram our thought life and to help us forgive those we think have made us ungovernable. Forgive those you believe have impacted your life so negatively that it has made you want to impact others negatively as well.

I can imagine what is going through your mind. I agree—

talk is cheap, and action is a hard bone to chew. It may be, but if you keep at it consistently, chewing bit by bit, with time there will be no piece of the bone left. Mission accomplished!

As you gaze at God, he reproduces his character in you. He continues to fill you with his spirit, as you spend time with him and his word. The more he fills you, the less you give in to the influence of the immature culture around you. The shackles and the chains of the life suckers are broken, and you are free to believe, live and give.

Believe in who you are called to be, even if you don't see it yet. Work towards who you are (for your maker speaks of things not in existence as though they are) even if you don't see it yet. Someday you will look back and realize that indeed, you are transformed.

If you are single now or called to be single, embrace it and make the most of it. Refuse to be pressured otherwise. Refuse to react negatively to where you are now. Go through singlehood gracefully, and savour every moment.

CHAPTER SIX

Things to do, places to go!

Life is an adventure! If you are on the sideline waiting, you miss out! Plunge in and you will be fulfilled!

Bury the self-consuming mindset, for there are places to go and things to do; the world beckons. Surely you have something to offer the world. The world is seeking people of influence, people the world can look up to, people to proffer solutions— and you are one of them. You have something to contribute. Do not take that lightly. Do not let the myths and the abnormalities of society cause you to swerve away from your destiny.

You are not here on earth for you. You are here for what transcends you. Discover that and channel your time and energy into it.

The right man for you may come. When he does, because you know your mission, you will choose a man who will support you. In fact, you will support each other.

God is shaping every detail of your life—every experience and every challenge will work out for your good.

For those of you who hope to marry someday, the period of waiting does not diminish you. Rather, you are enlarged because you maximized your phase as a single woman. If you find a husband, you will have enjoyed both worlds: your single life and then your married life. When you marry right, you will have fewer regrets because you will have spent time knowing yourself and what you want, your likes and dislikes, what you can cope with or accommodate, and what you cannot cope with or accommodate. Your singleness will have matured you, so that you can handle the challenges that relationships bring.

I got a doctoral degree in 2012, and I have about 27 publications. This is a 'wow' for some people, but not for me. I certainly appreciate the progress I have made, but if people had just a little idea of my dreams, they would know that I have not accomplished a fifth of them. I see being single as an opportunity to press on with those dreams. Granted, my present job (faculty at a university) is so demanding that it gives little room for other pursuits. Prioritization is helpful; it also helps to have a routine and to get rid of distractions.

In September of 2014, I decided to try having a routine. There were three things that had been craving for my attention, and I had been using the excuse of work not to get them done. As I was away at another laboratory for some research, I decided it might be good to get into a routine. I had heard it said that habits form if the action is executed faithfully for 21 days. If these routines become habits while I was away from my place of work, I was hoping that by the time I got back, I could continue with them.

So I decided to tackle those three things. First, due to the sedentary nature of my work, I had become slightly overweight. A bit of routine exercise would do me some good. I had tried a gym earlier, but I was never regular. Work ate into my gym time. So this time, I decided to exercise in the comfort of my home. No matter how tired I am when I get back from the laboratory, I do a bit of exercise, even if it is only for ten minutes.

I was sick for a week once, and I decided to rest, relax, eat, and recuperate. In a short time, I regained the 6kg I lost. The excuse of "I am sick, take it easy" earned me 6kg. Keeping fit has to be a routine that becomes part of me. I also learnt in the course of this routine that it is easier to add the weight than to lose it. So when I succeed in getting the fat out, the routine exercise will keep the fat away.

Secondly, I am a writer. I don't have to be an acclaimed writer to acknowledge that I am one. However, I never seem to be consistent. I started some blogs, and they have been deserted. Writing is something I enjoy, yet I don't get to do it. So I hope to make it a routine. I am trying to get up early in the mornings and write for one hour. I think it will be better than trying to write when I get back from work, when I am usually exhausted. I believe writing is an avenue for me to influence society.

I have a passion for women—I believe most of us are living below our capacity. A friend once said, "The church cannot be talking about restoration if women are not restored." We are called to be co-managers of this earth. We have roles to play. Each of us has a slice of God's purpose to fulfill on this earth. As I plunge into what I perceive is my assignment, I am convinced it will become clearer as I keep at it. I may make mistakes, but I will not, for fear of mistakes, decide not to take a plunge. One way of fulfilling this assignment is through writing. So I intend to use this single period to make a go of it.

Third, I seek to have intimacy with God. I want to fall into a routine of knowing God and daily spending quality time with him, a time not encumbered with thoughts of things not done or things to do. When I am with him, I want to shut down everything else. I perceive that this will help me to be cool, calm and collected as I face the challenges of each day.

What things have you always hoped you would accomplish? Consider using this period of singleness to accomplish them. Pick up your diary and make a list of things you would like to do. Which one is plausible to start as soon as possible? Now keep that diary so that you can refer to it occasionally.

41

Keep at it until you see yourself accomplishing all of them.

Do you want to buy a car? Do you want to buy a house? Do you want to go back to school? Do you want to start a hobby or business? What are those ideas bubbling in you? Make a go at them!

I would not be surprised if some women reading this come up blank. Many women have been schooled in a straitjacketed manner. *Get married and have children and keep the home!* So they have no other aspirations but these. When these don't get accomplished, they feel unsettled. You hear words like, "I need to settle down." If you are single, you are not unsettled. Open yourself to daring aspirations. Keep busy. Do things! Impact lives!

There are places to go. I enjoy traveling; this year, I plan to visit Mauritius. I want to learn about different cultures. It will help me to appreciate the diversities and similarities of other humans. Places to go? Make a list of them. What will it take to get your plans in motion? Funds are usually topmost. What expenses can you cut off to save for travel? You can start with one place or two a year. They don't have to cost a fortune. There may be affordable bed and breakfasts, or discounted tickets.

You can start by visiting places within your country. While I was in Johannesburg, two other women and I took a trip to Cape Town. It was then that I realized some people living in Johannesburg have never been to Cape Town. You can start by visiting neighboring states, provinces, districts, or countries. Trust me—the effects and exposure cannot be quantified!

If you are planning to re-invent yourself, don't just do a body makeover. Add doing things and visiting places; for they do the soul a whole lot of good.

CHAPTER SEVEN

Complete and not lonely

I was made fabulous, and I understand who I am.

Relationships do us a lot of good; there is no doubt about that. Even if you don't have the intimate relationship of marriage, do not shut yourself out of other relationships. I am single, but I have male friends who I enjoy. I still get male perspectives about things. Some may say it is not the same—what about sex?

For those who believe that sex is only appropriate in the confines of marriage, it will be a concern. Yes, sex confined to marriage is the norm, even though society considers it abnormal. My friend once said, "What you have never tasted or experienced, you don't miss." Is it possible to do without sex, even if you have experienced it? Yes, it is possible, but it will take discipline. A single woman can be complete and not lonely without an intimate relationship. Christ becomes her sustenance.

When I was at the university, religious men would tell us to marry so we could be complete. They said that a woman is incomplete without her other half. Some people still believe this doctrine. For some, the only issue they present to God is marriage, for 'it is not good for me to be alone'. This trans-generational 'doctrine,' which has persisted for centuries, puts women under tremendous pressure to get married. Girls grow up being told that marriage is the ultimate goal and that she is made complete by marriage. This myth must give way to the truth. Neither the man nor the woman completes the other. A marriage is more successful if both the man and the woman come into the marriage already complete.

How can they become complete? Is that possible in this broken world of ours? Yes—in Christ, we are all complete! To be complete means having it all, entire and lacking nothing. On our own it is not possible. Even when a woman marries, wholeness is not conferred on her. Her completeness or wholeness is in Christ.

Is it possible some broken marriages are as a result of misplaced expectations? The wife seeks in her husband what only God can do for her. You don't need a man to be complete. Being complete is a choice. Christ makes us whole. So we choose to align with him and to accept what he has done. He laid down his life; he shed his blood so our broken lives may be made whole. When we make our home with him, and he makes his home with us, we are made whole. In him we live, move and have our being. Marriage is good, but even if you remain single, you are still complete. For you come into the fullness of life in Christ. I am complete in Christ, and I have no doubt about it.

It is possible to be alone and not lonely. Do I deny that loneliness exists? No! It does exist. However, the impact of loneliness is more when you are idle. Loneliness is the result of negative self-assessment. If you are physically sound and there was no tragic loss from which you are still recovering, then loneliness is an internal perception you must trash. Anyone who continues to sail on the boat of loneliness has chosen to do so. You can get off the boat with your own two legs. When your heart signals you to move out of the boat of loneliness, don't choose to linger on. Get off the boat!

I am so busy that there is no space for loneliness in my mind. Right now I am taking two online courses, I have my full-time job, and I am honing my writing. I'm busy from morning till night. However, I am trying to work towards keeping my weekends freer. One of the online courses— *Better Leader, Richer Life*—is to help me achieve the desired four-way win at the four domains of my life: work, home, community, and self.

Right now, work gets 70% of my attention while self gets 30%. That must change! There is simply no room in my life for loneliness. When I was less busy and delayed in taking up my postgraduate program, I started blogging. I attended several workshops and seminars for career development. I refused to mourn the delay; rather, I maximized it.

For me, once I sense loneliness, I know there has been a disconnection between Christ and me. Being supportive and encouraging to others not only uplifts others but also uplifts you in the process. Combat loneliness by changing your thought patterns, practicing contentment, keeping yourself busy, and attending to other people's needs.

My community awaits me! Your community awaits you! Let's step out and enlarge our sphere of influence.

It is normal to be single. It should be acceptable to be single. If a woman does not meet Mr. Right early, she should not be pressured against her judgment to marry Mr. Wrong. If she is comfortable being single, she should not be pressured into thinking it is abnormal.

Marriage is lovely; singleness is equally lovely. Singleness is a gift and a calling, and it should be appreciated. If a woman chooses to be single, she should be respected and supported. If she has been called to be single, she should not be pressured to go contrary to her calling. I appreciate my family and some of my friends who have accepted me for what I am—a single woman. I am not certain what the future holds; however, I intend to savour the present moment and live it to the full.

Can singles be complete and not lonely? Yes, we can! Kick out the life suckers, do the things, go to the places,

and mingle with positive influencers. Make a positive impact, and you will discover that it is possible to be single and complete, alone and content!

Acknowledgments

This book would not have been without the inspiration of Professor Nelson Ochekpe. I would like to thank Daisi and Cecy Alabi for their suggestions and for accepting for who I am – a single lady. I appreciate the valuable inputs from my beta readers: my sister [Ngozi Nwoke], Nelson Ochekpe, Daisi Alabi and my pastor, Dotun Reju, who also wrote the foreword. Thank you to Jan Ackerson for making an exception to edit this book. I appreciate her commitment, valuable suggestions and editing. It was a delight interacting with her.

www.ingramcontent.com/pod-product-compliance
Lightning Source LLC
Chambersburg PA
CBHW031008090426
42737CB00008B/728